life and a religious observance of the siesta. The Sevillian's most joyful side is to be seen during the April Fair, whilst Holy Week is when the city's inhabitants reveal the matching depth of their piety.

The pages of this guide contain a number of routes organised to help visitors make the most of their stay here. Each is preceded by a plan showing the different sights it describes. The first route is dedicated to the most monumental zone of the city, basically the cathedral and the Reales Alcázares. The second, from the Santa Cruz district to the House of Pilate, reveals more of the customs of Seville. The third takes in the more commercial part of the city, as well as the Macarena, San Vicente and San Lorenzo districts, whilst the fourth introduces us to the Seville which lives by the river, and the working-class Triana district. The fifth route conducts us from the Jerez Gate to María Luisa Park, a built-up area outside the walls of the old city. Finally, the sixth route takes us to "Isla de la Cartuja", on the other side of the river. This book also contains an overall plan of Seville, as well as opening with sections devoted to the city's history, festivities, food and drink and crafts.

Aerial view of the old town.

INTRODUCTION

The city of Seville stands on the plains of the River Guadalquivir, in the south-west of the Iberian Peninsula. The area enjoys a benign, predominantly Mediterranean, climate, with mild winters, pleasant temperatures in spring and autumn, and long, hot summers. With a population that has now surpassed the 700,000 mark, the city is the capital of both Seville province and of the Autonomous Community of Andalusia.

Since its foundation, attributed to Hercules and also linked to the mythical Tartessos, Seville has enjoyed various moments of great splendour. Roman Seville was magnificent, though little trace of the period remains. The city acquired particular importance after 45 BC, when Julius Caesar granted it the status of colony and made it the capital of Bética. (Betis is the name the Romans gave to the River Guadalquivir). Ancient Hispalis, as it had been known even before the times of the Romans, then became the political, economic and administrative capital of the south of the Peninsula and North Africa.

The most important remains from the Roman period are found in **Italica**, some ten kilometres from the city centre. This is a Roman city founded in the year 206 BC by Scipio Africanus as a site for his troops to withdraw to after the victory over the Carthaginian general Hasdrubal in a battle which took place nearby. Over the years, Italica became a prosperous urban centre. The ruins we can now visit still show the layout of the city, as well as remains

GUIDE TO
SEVILLE

Photographs: Jorge Toledo and
FISA-Escudo de Oro Photographic Archives.

Text, design, lay-out and printing completely created
by the technical department of
EDITORIAL FISA ESCUDO DE ORO S.A.

 ESCUDO DE ORO

THE VISIT TO SEVILLE

Some cities have more monuments than one can reasonably hope to visit. Such is the case of Seville, a city which begs to really *lived*, experienced, not merely visited, for, besides its rich historic heritage, its vital magic also exerts a powerful attraction on the visitor. Seville is a cosmopolitan, international city, but one which is also reticent towards change, rightly proud of its glorious past. The people of Seville are open, cheerful, extrovert, charming in their way of speaking and doing things, with a relaxed, pleasure-seeking approach to life, a love of the night-

of mosaics and sculptures, but particularly impressive are the theatre and amphitheatre, this last elliptical in shape and holding 25,000 spectators.

Under the Visigoths, Seville once more attained the status of leading cultural

centre of the Western world. Saint Isidore of Seville (560-636), the author of *The Etymologies*, which

contains all the knowledge of the time, was the city's greatest figure. The Visigoth period was followed by another time of splendour: Islamic Seville. The Moors knew the city as *Isbiliah* and the river as

Roman ruins of Italica.

SAINTS JUSTA AND RUFINA

Our first news of a Christian community in Seville comes from Justa and Rufina, the city's patron saints. Sisters, they ran a crockery stall en Triana. However, in around the year 287 AD, they refused to make a donation for a pagan procession, confessing their faith. When the crowd smashed their glasses, the sisters destroyed the pagan idol, for which they were martyred. Great artists such as Murillo, Zurbarán and Goya all found inspiration in this story, and the Giralda tower is often represented in depictions of the sisters as, according to legend, they saved it from destruction in the 1755 earthquake. The feast of saints Justa and Rufina is July 19.

"Saints Justa and Rufina", by Goya in 1817 (Seville Cathedral).

"St Isidore", a work by Murillo in 1655 (Seville Cathedral).

the *Guad El Kevir* ("the great river"), from which expressions their modern names are derived. Under Moorish domination from 712 to 1248, Seville emerged as one of the principal cities in Al-Andalus. Its urban layout was defined during this period, much of it conserved to this day, and the city walls were built to protect it. Moreover, great buildings such as the Mosque and the Giralda, the tower which served as its minaret, were constructed.

After two years of siege, in 1248 Ferdinand III, the Holy, finally took Seville. The Moors were expelled, with the exception of converts, whilst the Jews were, for the moment, left in peace (they were expelled from Spain in 1492) and the city was repopulated by "colonists" from Castile. However, the tolerant rule of King Alphonse X, the Wise, permitted the development of the Jewish, Arabic and Christian cultures alike. The repopulation was accompanied by the division of Seville into districts by guild or foreign status, each with its own parish, and this prepared the ground for the phenomenon of the brotherhoods and guilds, the *hermandades* and *cofradías*. Seville was made capital of the Kingdom of Castile, its Moorish alcázar becoming the royal palace. Declared the City of God, in 1401 the construction of an extraordinary cathedral began on the site of the Great Mosque. The discovery of America brought with it a new period of splendour for Seville, as it was here that the Casa de Contratación ("Contracting House") was established, and with it a monopoly on trade with the New World. Converted into an imperial metropolis, the 16th and 17th centuries were the richest in the history of Seville and those which have left the greatest architectural wealth, with a particularly impressive number of baroque monuments. The terrible plague which struck the city in 1649 and the loss of the monopoly in trade with America to Cadiz in 1717 meant the beginning of decline for Seville, though the city struggled to retain the leading role it had played throughout its glorious history. The romantic ideals of the 19th century shared the cultural stage with a highly agitated political life. The city flourished somewhat under Isabel,

Portrait of Ferdinand III, the Holy, by Murillo (Seville Cathedral).

but it was above all with the organisation of the Spanish-American Exhibition of 1929 and, more recently, the 1992 Universal Exhibition, that Seville took on a new urban physiognomy and began to look to the future with hope. Nevertheless, this new Seville co-exists harmoniously with the historic city, the Seville which was successively Roman, Moorish-Andalusian and baroque.

NO8DO

The peculiar emblem that we can see in nooks and crannies all over Seville and on various versions of the city coat of arms is attributed to Alphonse X. It features the cryptogram or city logo NO8DO, formed by two syllables joined by an image resembling a skein of yarn ("madeja"), the phonetic expression of the phrase "no me ha dejado" ("she did not abandon me"). This is a reference to the loyalty the city showed to Alphonse when the king entered into conflict with his son, Don Sancho.

FESTIVITIES

Holy Week in Seville is a unique spectacle, reaching heights of intensity and emotion that the visitor can only understand by sharing it with the people of the city. For the Sevillian, this is the great *fiesta*, the most popular, pure passion. Its origins go back to the 16th century, and there now exist around 50 *cofradías*, or brotherhoods, which parade a total of around one hundred *pasos*, floats, in the processions. These take place every day during Holy Week, with the participation

Holy Week.

of seven or eight brotherhoods each day, continuing well into the night to complete their route. Programmes are sold in the streets and local newspapers provide timetables, routes and other information.

The processions begin in the churches where the brotherhoods have their headquarters. From there, they go to the cathedral and back again, taking different routes. Each brother-

The April Fair.

hood, all of which have different costumes, usually carries two *pasos*, sculptural groups, the first representing an image of the Passion and the second a *Dolorosa*, or statue of the Virgin affected by the pain of the death of Jesus. These floats are carried on the shoulders of the *costaleros* to a rhythm marked by the voice of a *capataz*. The penitents accompanying the floats wear hoods on their heads and carry candles in their hands. The carvings are often veritable works of art, most dating to the 17th century, the figures richly dressed and adorned, particularly the representations of Our Lady. All this helps to generate a spectacular atmosphere, together with the crowds which gather and the aroma of flowers, incense and candles.

After the solemnity of Holy Week, the city explodes into joy during the **April Fair**. This fair takes place during the second half of April and lasts one week. *La Feria de Abril*, as it is known, is a secular, country-style festivity which was first staged in 1848, though its origins go back to a cattle market which used to be held here. The Fair is installed in Prado de San Sebastián, where a great entrance archway lit up by hundreds of light bulbs beckons us into an enclosure full of canvas marquees put up by the different associations which take part. Inside, the fun and dancing of *Sevillanas* goes on to the early

The Dance of the Sixes, or "Seises".

hours, whilst outside horsemen parade their ornately-harnessed steeds and women wear their finest dresses, forming a unique and colourful spectacle. During **Corpus Christi**, which takes place at the end of May or during the first fortnight of June, a procession starts out from the cathedral and goes around some of the streets of the city centre, led by Juan de Arfe's great processional monstrance, followed by various *pasos* and representatives from Sevillian civil and religious society. The events also feature the dances of the *Seises* ("sixes") before the high altar in the cathedral. The dance resembles a slow minuet and is performed by young people dressed in typical 17th-century costumes.

The pilgrimage known as the **Romería del Rocío** takes place at Whitsun. This traditional event has taken place since the early-18th century, and the pilgrimage is made by Sevillians and vis-

itors alike, culminating at the Chapel of El Rocío near Almonte (Huelva). The journey from Seville covers 95 kilometres and is made in carts pulled by oxen, on horseback or on foot. Well-organised groups accompany and escort the *Carro del Sinpecado* ("cart of the Sinless One") which identifies each brotherhood. The procession reaches the chapel on Whit Saturday and the offering is made to the Virgin, popularly known as *La Blanca Paloma* ("The White Dove"), faithfully watched over by the Matriz de Almonte brotherhood. On the Sunday, a solemn mass is held, and at night a public rosary takes place. In the early hours of Monday morning, the people of Almonte, the only ones so privileged, jump over the grille and carry the statue of the Virgin out in procession. As one, the multitude acclaims the Virgin, crowding round to try to touch the silver poles of the float.

The Romería del Rocío procession.

Gazpacho, cakes and pastries, and olives.

FOOD AND DRINK

When it comes to gastronomic delights, the Sevillian people are fond, above all, of eating "tapas" and of the "chateo", doing the rounds of the bars. This love for taking a bite to eat and

a drink here and there is usually shared with friends, for it inevitably involves bumping into different groups of acquaintances in each establishment visited. The variety of tapas available in Seville is enormous, ranging from exquisite local olives to fried fish, not forgetting small fillets of beef, *solda-ditos de Pavía* (small pieces of cod fried in flour), croquettes and bull's tail. The most popular dishes in Sevillian cuisine are *gazpacho* (a refreshing cold soup) and *cocido andaluz* (stew), a much denser, baroque affair. The local sweets and pastries include many products made at convents and monasteries, such as the renowned "yemas de San Leandro", "bollitos de Santa Inés" and the sweet jams from the Convent of Santa Paula.

Soldaditos de Pavía, boquerones (anchovies), calamares (squid) and rabo de toro (bull's tail).

ARTS AND CRAFTS

There are still many craft workshops in Seville, their methods practically unchanged over the centuries, thanks mainly to the demand produced by activities related to the different guilds and brotherhoods. The local embroidery techniques, using silk, gold, silver and copper thread, go back to the 15th cen-

tury, when a guild is recorded as working in this art. Sevillian gold and silverwork has also produced brilliant pieces, of which the monstrance known as the Custodia de Arfe is the most outstanding masterpiece, but the whole city also testifies to the skill of its smiths, boasting countless artistic grilles. Ceramic-work is another activity which has had great importance here since earliest times. Here, one of the most characteristic elements are altarpieces covered in *azulejos*, glazed tiles, in the outer walls of churches, representing the image to be found in the interior. Other important local crafts include carving and gilding, and the city has produced many masters throughout its history.

17

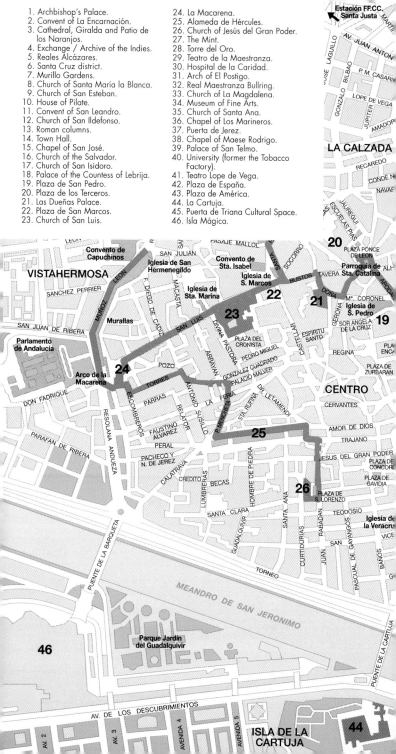

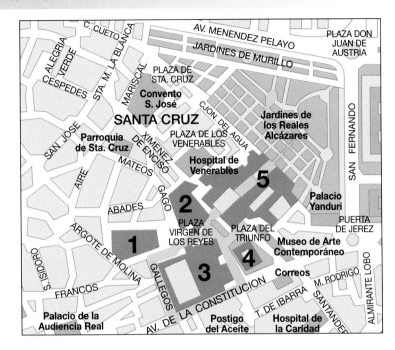

1. FROM THE CATHEDRAL TO THE REALES ALCÁZARES

1.- Archbishop's Palace. 2.- Convent of La Encarnación. 3.- Cathedral, Giralda and Patio de los Naranjos. 4.- Exchange / Archive of the Indies. 5.- Reales Alcázares.

We begin this first itinerary in the **Plaza Virgen de los Reyes**, the heart of monumental Seville, as the magnificent buildings it contains form a historic and artistic compendium of the city. On one side are the rear of the cathedral, the Giralda and part of the walls of the Patio de los Naranjos, whilst opposite is the Archbishop's Palace and at a third corner stands the Convent of La Encarnación. In the centre of the square are a fountain and a spectacular lamppost.

Plaza de la Virgen de los Reyes.

The **Archbishop's Palace (1)** has a lovely front, created by Lorenzo Fernández in the 18th century. With its deep colours (blood red and ochre yellow) and the graceful rhythms of its elements, this is a fine exponent of the Sevillian façade at the pinnacle of baroque splendour in the city. Inside the palace are a staircase of jasper and an excellent collection of paintings by Zurbarán, Murillo, Herrera the Elder and Valdés Leal, amongst others. Moreover, recent restoration led to the unearthing of the ruins of Roman and Moorish baths here.

Opposite the Archbishop's Palace is the contrasting white edifice of the **Convent of La Encarnación (2),** which began to be built in the 14th century, but of which only the church remains. Adjoining it, a side street leads to the recondite **Plaza de Santa Marta**. The centre of this charming square, sur-

Archbishop's Palace.

rounded by orange trees and whitewashed houses adorned by wrought-iron grilles and geraniums, features a simple stone cross.

Plaza de Santa Marta.

The Giralda and a partial view of the Giraldillo.

Nearby Calle Maetos Gago commands a fine view of the **Giralda (3)**, though, in fact, this tower is a landmark that can be seen from all over the city. The Giralda is the best-known symbol of the city and one of the most greatly admired towers in the world. It was built by the Almohades over Roman remains in the 12th century as the minaret to the Great Mosque, on the site where the cathedral the now stands. The tower was then crowned by four great golden spheres which, however, fell off during the 1356 earthquake. The Giralda is now crowned by a bell chamber arranged in diminishing sections or kiosks, the work of Hernán Ruiz. The final section began to be built in 1558. At the very top is an enormous statue representing the Triumph of Faith in the form of a weathercock which soon became known as El Giraldillo, the name from which that of the tower is derived. Inside, 35 gentle ramps lead up to a splendid viewpoint over the city, at a height of 70 metres. The total height of the tower is almost 100 metres.

Before entering the **Cathedral (3)** itself, a walk around the surrounding streets will give us an idea of the size of the site, for we are before the largest in Spain and one of the biggest in the world: 130 metres in length and 76 in width, with the highest point of the crossing reaching 56 metres. The greater part of the cathedral was constructed between 1420 and 1506, and features Gothic, neo-Gothic and Renaissance elements. The dome, which collapsed in 1511, was rebuilt in 1519 and was completely restored once

Two views of the Giralda, the former minaret.

THE CATHEDRAL STEPS

The so-called gradas or Cathedral steps were built in 1392, after a very difficult year in the countryside, as a place where workers could be hired, but soon became frequently used as a forum for all kinds of commercial transactions, particularly after the discovery of America. People from all walks of life and places came here to seek work or strike business deals that they would later formalise at the Casa de la Contratación, near the Reales Alcázares. On rainy or excessively hot days, many continued their business inside the cathedral, a tendency the Chapter sought to counter by installing chains all round the building. The problem was finally resolved, however in 1572, when the exchange, or Casa Lonja de Mercaderes (now the Archive of the Indies) was built. The chains also marked the limits of the sanctuary that existed outside as well as inside the cathedral, a right that continued to exist until fairly recently.

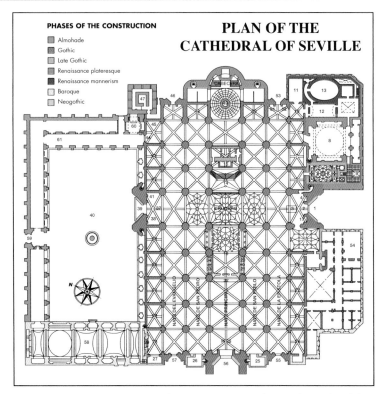

PLAN OF THE CATHEDRAL OF SEVILLE

PHASES OF THE CONSTRUCTION
- Almohade
- Gothic
- Late Gothic
- Renaissance plateresque
- Renaissance mannerism
- Baroque
- Neogothic

1- Prince's Door. 2- Southern Arm of the crossing. 3- Culumbus' Tomb. 4- Altar of the Piedad. 5- Chapel of Dolores. 6- Sacristy of the Chalices. 7- San Andres' Chapel 8- Main Sacristy. 9- Patio of the Casa de Cuentas. 10- Marshal's Chapel. 11- Room of the Ornaments. 12- Antechapter. 13- Chapterhouse Room. 14- Main Chapel. 15- Main Retable. 16- Choir. 17- Concepción's Altar. 18- Chapel of the Antigua. 19- San Hermenegildo's Chapel. 20- Concepción Chica's Chapel. 21- Encarnación's Chapel. 22- San Jose's Chapel. 23- Santa Ana's Chapel. 24- San Laureano's Chapel. 25- San Isidoro's Chapel. 26- San Leandro's Chapel. 27- Chapel of the Angustias. 28- Replica of the Giraldillo. 29- Facade of the Sagrario's church. 30- San Antonio's Chapel. 31- Chapel of Nuestra Señora de la Consolación de los Doce Apóstoles. 32- Transchoir. 33- Chapel of the Star (Capilla de la Estrella). 34- Chapel of San Gregorio. 35- Santiago's Chapel. 36- San Francisco's Chapel. 37- Northern arm of the Crossing. 38- Chapel of Bethlehem. 39- Door of the Concepción. 40- Patio of the Orange Trees. 41- Asunción's Altar. 42- Chapel of the Maidens. 43- Chapel of the Evangelists. 44- Door of the Lizard. 45- Pilar's Chapel. 46- Door of the Stakes (Puerta de los Palos). 47- Giralda. 48- San Pedro's Chapel. 49- Royal Chapel. 50- Chapel of the Concepción Grande. 51- Santa Barbara's Altar. 52- Altar of the Santas Justa and Rufina. 53- Door of the Little Bells. 54- Archive and Offices. 55- Door of the Crib. 6- Asunción's Door. 57- Door of the Baptism. 58- Sagrario's Church. 59- Door of the Forgiveness. 60- Virgin of the Granada's Chapel. 61- Chapterhouse and Colombina Library.

Aerial view of the cathedral.
The cathedral, seen from Plaza del Triunfo.

more after the 1888 earthquake. All around the building are the well-known *gradas*, steps, protected by a belt of chains and columns, since the cathedral's origins a place for trade and the hiring of labour, as well as a meeting-point and a place of refuge.

The main façade of the cathedral, in Avenida de la Constitución, has three doors: the main door, also known as that of the Assumption, and dating to the 19th century, and those of the Baptistery and the Birth, both built in the 15th century and profusely decorated with terra cotta figures. In the south side is the Door of San Cristóbal, completed in the 19th century, whilst the rear front features, on either side of the Gothic apse, the doors of Las Campanillas and Los Palos, this last adjoining the

The portals of El Príncipe, La Campanilla and Los Palos.

Giralda. Both are by Perrín in Gothic style with Renaissance elements. The north wall contains one of the most interesting of the cathedral doors, the Puerta del Perdón, or Pardon Door. This dates back to the Almohade period, as the two great bronze door panels, finely decorated with tracery and bearing Kufic inscriptions, testify. The sculptures of Saint Peter and Saint Paul in the 16th-century Annunciation group are by Miguel Florentín, and the Plateresque plaster decoration, which also dates to the 16th century, is by Bartolomé López.

The Puerta del Perdón leads into the **Patio de los Naranjos (3),** formerly

The Pardon Door, or Puerta del Perdón.

Patio de los Naranjos.

the *sahn* or patio of ablutions of the Great Mosque. This peaceful garden, perfumed by the aroma of orange blossom, is surprising in its simple beauty. It has a central fountain whose bowl comes from a former Visigoth cathedral, and a stone pulpit from which preached, amongst others, John of Avila, Francis of Borja and Vincent Ferrer. Hanging in the so-called Aisle of El Lagarto is a full-scale copy of a crocodile whose original is said to have been a gift from the Sultan of Egypt to King Alphonse X, the Wise. Over this aisle is the Columbine Library, founded in 1551, and which contains an enormous and priceless collection of manuscripts donated by the son of Christopher Columbus. On the west is the cathedral Chapel of El Sagrario, built in the 17th century and now an independent parish church. The church contains an altarpiece on the theme of the Descent from the Cross featuring sculptures by Pedro Roldán, impressive in their realism, and colossal statues of the Evan-

gelists and the Fathers of the Church, by Juan de Arce.

The Puerta de Oriente (East Door), also known as that of Los Naranjos or of La Concepción, built in the 20th century in the Gothic style, and the Puerta del Lagarto both lead into the cathedral. On entering, the impression we receive is almost overwhelming, as we are moved by the grandeur and power of the building. The cathedral has a nave and four aisles with 30 chapels. This magnificent site contains a wealth of art works by some of the outstanding figures in the history of art.

In the nave, passing the choir and retrochoir, the former featuring splendid Gothic choirstalls and 17th-century organs, is the Capilla Mayor, or Chapel High, enclosed behind a fine 16th-century Plateresque grille of gilt iron. Presiding over it is an immense altarpiece, a masterpiece of Flamboyant Gothic and one of the cathedral's most precious treasures. This colossal altarpiece, measuring some 20 metres high by 13 wide, the largest in the Christian world, was worked on by practically all the city's artists. The original design is by Pierre Dancart and was executed between 1482 and 1533. It contains a total of 45 panels with over

Painting by Zurbarán, in the Chapel of San Pedro.

Cathedral: choir.

one thousand figures depicting scenes from the Old and New Testaments. The Virgen de la Sede, a 14th-century Gothic carving of Our Lady, occupies a place of honour in this monumental work.

In contrast with the rest of the cathedral, the Capilla Real is Renaissance-Plateresque in style, with a fine coffered dome designed by Hernán Ruiz. It contains the tombs of Alphonse X, the Wise, and his mother, Beatrice of Schwaben, and, in a magnificent silver urn, the mortal remains of the sainted King Ferdinand the Holy. Moreover, in the crypt at the rear of the chapel

Altarpiece in the Chapel High: overall view, with the grille, and partial view.

The Royal Chapel.

Urn of Saint Ferdinand.

are the tombs of Peter the Cruel and his wife, Maria of Padilla. Presiding the altar is a 13th-century statue of the Virgen de los Reyes (Our Lady of Kings), patron saint of Seville. Early in the morning every August 15, this carving, venerated locally, is carried in procession through the streets around the cathedral before a silent multitude which gathers to watch Her go by. According to the "tradition of the three graces", the Virgin grants the three wishes She is asked as Her statue is brought out. The Sacristía Mayor,

Statue of Our Lady (La Virgen de los Reyes).

or High Sacristy, which forms part of the cathedral museum, contains the magnificent cathedral treasure, whose riches include a colossal candelabra by Morel and Hernán Ruiz, and the huge processional monstrance by Juan de Arfe, a unique example of Renaissance silverwork. This exquisite treasure leads the procession during Corpus Christi, when the traditional dance of the "Seises" ("Sixes") is performed before the high altar.

The Sacristy of Los Cálices, reached through the Chapel of Los Dolores, boasts paintings by Goya, Zurbarán and Valdés Leal, whilst the altar is presided over by one of the finest exponents of Sevil-

High Sacristy: "Descent from the Cross", by Pedro de Campaña in 1548.

lian baroque religious sculpture, the Cristo de la Clemencia, by Martínez Montañés in 1603.

Opposite the Door of San Cristóbal is the mausoleum dedicated to Christopher Columbus, a composition by Arturo Melida in 1900 in which the tomb is born by four pages with the escutcheons of Castile, Navarre, León and Aragon.

Nearby **Plaza del Triunfo** also contains a number of outstanding monuments: the cathedral, the palace which now houses the offices of the provincial government, or Diputación, the walls of

the Reales Alcázares and the Archivo General de Indias, or "Archive of the Indies". The square takes its name from the **Monument to Triumph**, erected to commemorate the All Saints' Mass that was interrupted by the earthquake

The monstrance known as the Custodia de Arfe.

Mausoleum of Christopher Columbus.

Monument to La Inmaculada.

of 1755, and which devastated much of the city. The **monument to La Inmaculada**, in the centre of the square, is by Collaut Valera and was installed here on the occasion of the proclamation of the dogma of the Immaculate Conception.

The **Archivo General de Indias (Archive of the Indies, 4)** is in austere Renaissance style. The square building has two storeys and a porticoed central courtyard. It was built between 1584 and 1598 by Juan de Herrera to house the former Exchange, or *Lonja de Mercaderes*, in order to decongest the intense trading activity in the nearby *Casa de la Contratación* and on the steps of the cathedral after the discovery of America. As the seat

General Archive of the Indies: façade giving onto Plaza del Triunfo.

SEVILLE BY CARRIAGE OR BOAT

Typical local horse-drawn carriages can usually be found in Plaza Virgen de los Reyes and Plaza del Triunfo, the horses often brightly adorned. This is the most traditional and delightful way of touring the city, though the route is more restricted these days. Another possibility is to take one of the bus tours offered by different agencies, whilst boat trips along the River Guadalquivir are another charming way of seeing Seville, particularly in the early evening. Boats depart from the mooring area beside the Torre del Oro.

General Archive of the Indies: main façade.

of the India Archives, it was founded in 1785 by King Charles III to centralise extensive and invaluable documentation relating to the New World, previously distributed amongst various different institutions. It now houses one of the most important libraries in the world.

Opposite, in Calle Santo Tomás, stands a building of similar characteristics, dating back to the 18th century. This is the former Casa del Diezmo, now the **Museum of Contemporary Art.**

The **Reales Alcázares Sevillanos (5)** are known in the plural because the site is made up of a number of buildings, from the original Moorish Alcázar palace to later extensions in the form of courtyards and palaces

carried out by different monarchs. Of the Alcázar built by the Almohades in the 12th century, all that remains is part of the walls and two courtyards: the Patio del Yeso and the Patio de la Montería. Its actual structure corresponds largely to the alterations carried out by King Peter I who, nevertheless, used many elements from the original construction.

We enter the Alcázares through the Lion Gate, or Puerta del León, opened in the Almohade walls from Plaza del Triunfo. To the left is the Chamber of Justice, which survives from the Alcázar

Puerta del León: overall view of this Lion Gate, and partial view of the glazed tile from which it takes its name.

Patio de la Montería.

created by Alphonse XI, adjoining the Patio del Yeso. Next we come to the Patio de la Montería, the *mexuar* of the Moorish building, a kind of antechamber separating the city from the palace proper. The original Alcázar followed the classical design of Moorish palaces, with an area for public life around the Patio de las Doncellas, and a second area reserved for private life,

Partial view of the coffering in the Justice Chamber.

Oratory of the Catholic Monarchs, and the azulejo glazed tiles by Niculoso Pizano.

the dependencies of which are built around the Patio de las Muñecas. The site was completed by extensive walled gardens.

Giving onto the Patio de la Montería is the impressive façade of the Palace of King Don Pedro, a masterpiece of Mudejar art. It was built in the 14th century by local artists and Nasrite craftsmen brought here from Granada, as well as carpenters from Toledo. It is exquisitely decorated, with Kufic and Gothic inscriptions, bearing witness to the blending of cultures which took place in those days. Of the various dependencies on the upper floor, outstanding is the so-called Oratorium of the Catholic Monarchs, a small chapel whose tiled altar, by Niculoso Pisano in 1503, is a key piece in Sevillian ceramics, representing an innovation in the art of tile-making.

From the Patio de la Montería, a marbled columned vestibule leads to the renowned Patio de las Doncellas,

large and full of light. Its walls are also covered by tiles, without a doubt the most beautiful in the entire palace. The upper floor was added in the 14th century, unfortunately spoiling some of the

Patio de las Doncellas.

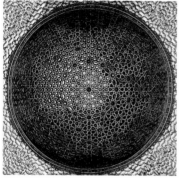

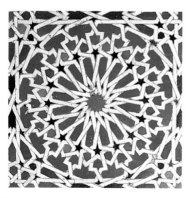

Salón de Embajadores: overall view of this Hall of Ambassadors, partial view of the dome and glazed tiles.

stylised grace of the original courtyard. The fine columns are adorned with profuse plasterwork ornamentation. Also worthy of attention is the wooden coffering.

The Patio de las Doncellas communicates with the Charles V Room, which features magnificent Renaissance coffering. Next are the apartments of María de Padilla, wife of King Pedro. From here, we can enter either a dining room, which dates to the time of Ferdinand II, or the sumptuous Salón de Embajadores (Hall of the Ambassadors), the most admired room in the Alcázar. It was built under Pedro I and has survived practically unaltered to the present day, except for the addition of the balconies in the 16th century. The walls, arches and door frames are covered by fine Mudejar decoration, and

Altarpiece of La Virgen de los Mareantes, by Alejo Fernández (16th-century), in the Cuarto del Almirante.

Portrait in glazed tiles of the Emperor Charles V, by Cristóbal de Augusta (late-16th-century), in the Sala de los Azulejos.

Partial view of the Kings' Gallery. This room contains 56 panels painted by Diego de Esquivel between 1599 and 1600.

Patio de las Muñecas.

the room is crowned by a dome adorned with *mocarab* plasterwork originally from the 15th century, though subsequently restored on various occasions. The kings and queens represented in the Gallery of the Monarchs of Spain span from Recaredo to Philip II, who

Tapestry Room.

Gardens of the Reales Alcázares: overall view and Charles V Pavilion.

Gardens of the Reales Alcázares: Fountain of Mercury and door of Marchena.

transferred the capital from Seville to Madrid.

Through the Philip II Bedroom, we come to the Patio de las Muñecas, a courtyard of intimacy and a unique gracefulness around which the private life of the palace revolved. The base, the columns and the capitals are all original, whilst the upper section dates back to the 19th century. The courtyard

Parade ground, or Patio de Banderas.

communicates with the Isabel the Catholic Bedroom, the Prince's Room (where her only son, Don Juan, was born) and the Bedroom of the Moorish Kings, all of them finely-decorated apartments. A fine collection of Flemish tapestries is exhibited in the Charles V Rooms, at the other end of the palace.

The Alcázar gardens are one of the greatest attractions of this visit, however. Variously Moorish, Mudejar and Renaissance in design, they comprise an excellent exponent of an art at which the Andalusians are past masters. Over the centuries, the artistic beauty of the original gardens was further embellished by the addition of pavilions, fountains, statues and even a maze. Outstanding elements include

the great pool with the statue of Mercury, the Garden of the Dance, the adjoining Baths of María de Padilla, the Prince's Gardens, and the charming Charles V Pavilion, which features one of the most splendid coffered ceilings in the entire Alcázar. At one end of the gardened zone is the 16th-century Marchena Gate, brought here from another Sevillian palace. In the *apeadero*, a marble-columned room built in the 18th century, we can admire a collection of period carriages. Adjoining this room is the **Patio de Banderas**, an extensive space which serves as the Alcázar parade ground. One of its arches communicates with the nearby Santa Cruz district, marking the start of the next route described in this guide.

AZULEJO GLAZED TILES

The Reales Alcázares contain many fine examples of azulejos, glazed tiles, an art at which the Andalusians are past masters, and there are examples, in different forms and expression, all over the city. The Moors, who introduced the technique of making glazed tiles here, called it az-zulaij, meaning "the little brick", and it is from this term that the Spanish word derives. The craft of making glazed tiles became firmly established in Seville, particularly in the potter's shops of Triana. Whilst they were initially used to decorate interior walls, new industrial techniques now enable them also to be used for exteriors.

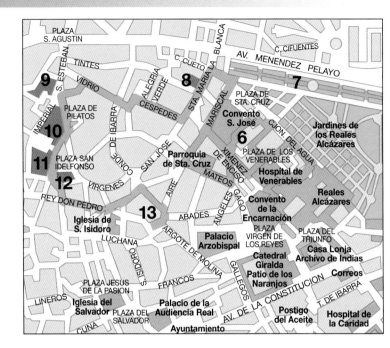

2. FROM THE SANTA CRUZ DISTRICT TO THE HOUSE OF PILATE

6.- Santa Cruz district. 7.- Murillo Gardens. 8.- Church of Santa María la Blanca. 9.- Church of San Esteban. 10.- House of Pilate. 11.- Convent of San Leandro. 12.- Church of San Ildefonso. 13.- Roman columns.

The **Santa Cruz district (6)** is, without doubt, the most colourful and characteristic in Seville. Its particular charm resides in its typical labyrinth of winding narrow streets, tiny squares and secret nooks and corners and in its light and the perfume in its air, filled with the scent of the many flowers tended in its patios and houses. All this combines to create a bewitching atmosphere, full of high drama and bursting with legends to seduce the visitor.

The district still conserves much of the form of what used to be the old Sevillian *aljama*, where, later, the Jewish community settled. However, part of its present physiognomy began to be acquired from the 16th century, when new squares were built and some streets widened. The style of the area was consolidated during the 19th century with the installation of wrought iron gates, making it possible to admire the inner courtyards of the houses from the street. To set out an itinerary or route through the streets of Santa Cruz seems almost an impossible task and perhaps the best way of getting to know its charms is

The Santa Cruz district: Calle de la Judería, Calle del Agua and Calle Gloria.

Two corners in Santa Cruz.

Plaza de Doña Elvira.

to lose oneself, just to follow one's feet. In any case, we can start our visit in the **Patio de Banderas**, which leads into **Calle de la Judería**. This street ends at the start of that known as **Calle de las Cadenas** ("Chain Street") in allusion to the chains supported by two columns here. According to the popular saying, "none who wish to marry should jump them". Calle de la Judería leads to **Calle Vida** and **Callejón del Agua**, this last parallel to the Alcázar walls and thus-known because of the water which ran along the wall.

The names of two streets, **Calle Pimienta** and **Calle de Susona**, evoke ancient legends, the second referring to the daughter of the rich Jew Susón. Susón was, it seems, the ringleader of a Jewish plot to take control of the city. His daughter, the lovely Susona, who had a clandestine romance with a Christian nobleman, warned her lover of the conspiracy in order to save his life. Her betrayal led to the execution of the conspirators and the repudiation of her family. On her death, as an exemplary punishment, Susona disposed that her head should

Plaza de los Venerables Sacerdotes.

fine fountain. Calle Gloria leads us to **Plaza de los Venerables Sacerdotes**, in which the former **Hospice of Los Venerables Sacerdotes** stands. This building, is one of the most outstanding baroque buildings in Seville, now houses the Focus cultural foundation. It was built between 1675 and 1695 according to plans drawn up by Leonardo Figueroa, and is decorated with paintings by Valdés Leal and his son Lucas Valdés. Calle Jamerdana and Calle Ximénez de Enciso lead us to **Calle Santa Teresa** where, at number 8, is the house where the artist Murillo died. Further on is the **Convent of San José**, a convent of Discalced Carmelites founded in the 17th century. **Plaza de Santa Cruz** opens up at the end of Calle Santa Teresa. This square was created during the period of French rule after the demolishment

be hung from the door. It is said that the skull remained there until the 18th century. A tile now commemorates this legend.

Calle Susona adjoins the romantic **Plaza de Doña Elvira**, a square presided over by orange trees and a

Hospital of Los Venerables Sacerdotes.

Plaza de Santa Cruz.

Murillo Gardens.

of the former Church of Santa Cruz where Murillo was buried, on a site previously occupied by a synagogue. In the centre of the square is the **Cruz de Cerrajería**, a splendid wrought iron cross dating to the year 1692. One end of the square communicates with **Plaza de los Refinaderos**, which is presided over by the statue of one of Seville's greatest figures, Don Juan Tenorio. The nearby **Calle de las Cruces** leads into the square of the same name, featuring three columns, each of them crowned by cross.

Nearby are the **Murillo Gardens (7)**, a broad expanse of green designed

Plaza de las Cruces.

SANTA CRUZ AND ITS PERSONALITIES

The Santa Cruz neighbourhood is linked to many celebrated personalities, both real, such as the painter Murillo, who was born and died here, and fictional, such as Don Juan Tenorio, though some authors consider that the legendary Sevillian philanderer was based on Don Miguel de Mañara, benefactor of the Charity Hospital. Don Juan was immortalised as a personality in the 17th century by the playwright Tirso de Molina, whose work later inspired other authors, from Zorrilla to Mozart, from Molière to Byron. Another writer, Washington Irving, who wrote the popular "Tales of the Alhambra" (1832), also had a house in the Santa Cruz neighbourhood, at number 2, Calle del Agua.

Monument to Don Juan Tenorio, in the Plaza de los Refinaderos.

by Juan Talavera in the early-20th century. The monument to Christopher Columbus, two columns featuring his caravels and crowned by a lion, is by Collaut Valera.

Calle Santa María la Blanca and Calle San José formerly marked the beginning of the old Jewish quarter of San Bartolomé. On the site where a synagogue used to stand is the **Church of Santa María la Blanca (8),** built in the 13th century, though extensively altered during the baroque period. The splendour of the works in this church makes it well worth a visit. Nearby, in the same street, is the **Palace of Altamira**, a superb 14th-century building with later additions, recently restored.

Taking Calle Céspedes, which runs through Plaza de las Mercedarias, Plaza del Vidrio and Plaza del Cristo del Buen Viaje, we come to **Plaza de San Esteban (9),** where the church of the same name stands. This is Mudejar in style and contains paintings by

Church of Santa María la Blanca.

Zurbarán and the sculpture of the seated Cristo de la Salud y Buen Viaje.

The **House of Pilate (10)** is a building of extraordinary interest due to its exquisite mixture of styles as varied as

House of Pilate: entrance.

the Mudejar, the Renaissance, the baroque and the Flamboyant Gothic. It was built at the command of Pedro Enríquez, governor of Andalusia, but its main promoter was his son, Don Fadrique, on his return from Jerusalem in 1519. The building's name is thought to be due either to the general impres-

House of Pilate: main courtyard.

House of Pilate: main staircase and partial view of a glazed tile.

sion that a copy was being built of the house of the infamous prefect of Judea, or that the palace was to be the first Station of the Cross (Christ Before Pilate) in a *via crucis* terminating at the former Cruz del Campo, a small church in the outskirts of the city.

The decorated marble portal, in the form of a triumphal arch, was built in Genoa

House of Pilate: the Praetor's Room.

in 1529. The beautiful main courtyard features an admirable mixture of styles: marble columns supporting arches decorated with Mudejar plasterwork; more Moorish features in the form of the tiled bands; the balustrades of the gallery featuring Gothic tracery; and Renaissance central fountain and layout of the patio. The friezes feature the busts of 24 Roman emperors and, in the four corners, three Roman goddesses and one Greek - Athena - an original piece dating back to the 5th century AD. Other rooms of particular interest are the Salón Dorado, or Gold Room (covered in gilt moulding), that of El Des-

House of Pilate: view of another room and the larger garden, or Jardín Grande.

canso de los Jueces ("Judges' Rest Room") with its tiled bands and the chapel leading into it (a combination of Gothic and Mudejar), the Gabinete de Pilatos (Mudejar fountain and coffered ceiling with central grotesque), and the staircase leading to the first floor, consisting of four flights and impressively decorated with colourful tiles. The upper floor contains a fine art collection. The House of Pilate also has two gardens, El Chico and El Grande, both of them an ideal setting for those wishing to relax in an atmosphere of peace and quiet.

Adjoining the House of Pilate is the **Convent of San Leandro (11),** which has become famous thanks to the delicious *yemas de San Leandro*, chief amongst Sevillian sweets and desserts. The convent dates to the 13th century, though the church was not built until the 17th. Inside it, the high altar is a fine exponent of Sevillian baroque art.

The main entrance to the **Church of San Ildefonso (12)** is in the nearby square of the same name. The building is easily recognisable thanks to the vivid colours of its stone and its baroque towers. Inside are works by such great Sevillian sculptors as Martínez Montañés and Pedro Roldán.

As we proceed now towards the city centre, a slight detour to Calle Mármoles will allow us to contemplate the few remains which survive, in a precarious state, from a temple built in the 2nd century by the Emperor Hadrian, of which only three **Roman columns (13)** survive. There were another three, but two were transferred to the Alameda de Hércules when this promenade was built, whilst the sixth was broken and lost.

Church of San Ildefonso.

The three Roman columns in Mármoles.

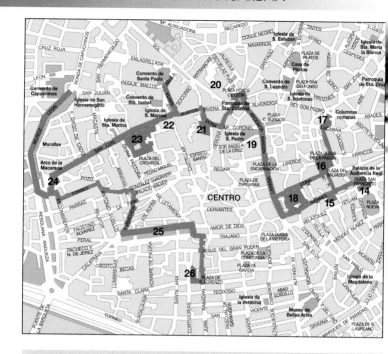

3. FROM THE CENTRE TO LA MACARENA

If Plaza de la Virgen de los Reyes is the monumental heart of Seville, **Plaza Nueva** and **Plaza de San Francisco** are its day-to-day, living heart, a role they share with nearby Calle de las Sierpes. Plaza Nueva is one of the city's most pleasant squares, dotted as it is with palm-trees and benches. In the centre of the square is an **equestrian statue of Saint Ferdinand** whilst half-hidden amongst the modern buildings is the **Chapel**

of San Onofre, the only remaining element from the great convent which occupied this site up until the mid-19th century.

Plaza de San Francisco has been a principal centre of the city since early times. Nevertheless, its present structure dates back to the alterations carried out during the first half of the 16th century, when the Town Hall was built, as were the fountain with the statue of the god Mercury, the

Plaza Nueva and the equestrian statue of Saint Ferdinand.

former Royal Prison, situated at the start of Calle de las Sierpes, and the Palace of the Royal Audience, now the offices of a savings bank. In the Middle Ages, the square was a business centre, the scene of tourneys and bullfights and a place for public executions during the time of the Inquisition, besides being a privileged space during Holy Week, as stands were erected here to enable the noble people of the city to watch the procession of all the brotherhoods and the Arfe monstrance for Corpus Christi. **The Town Hall** building **(14)** was designed by Diego de Riaño and has a fine Plateresque front. The arch known popularly as the "Arquillo" was built to provide entrance to the Convent of San Francisco, now lost. This arch is decorated with

The Fountain of Mercury (Plaza de San Francisco).

City Hall.

medallions and statues of Hercules and Julius Caesar, legendary founders of the city. The Town Hall contains such interesting rooms as the Chapter House, its ceiling formed by a flat vault with coffering adorned by portraits of various kings who ruled prior to the construction of the build-

La Campana, established in 1885, is one of the city's oldest cafés. We can find it at number 1, Calle de las Sierpes.

Two views of Calle de las Sierpes.

this street are a traditional meeting-point for Sevillians, and the zone has always been full of life and colour. Taking a stroll along this street and enjoying its many attractions is another way of getting to know Seville and its people.

From here to La Macarena, a fascinating, varied route takes us to visit several churches and palaces in the city. In Calle Jovellanos, adjoining Calle de las Sierpes, is the tiny **Chapel of San José (15)**, an excellent exponent of the most extreme of Sevillian baroque style. The **Parish Church of El Divino Salvador (16),** in Plaza del Salvador, is another outstanding example of works from the maximum period of splendour of the baroque style, its beauty only surpassed by the cathedral, such is the category of its superb altarpieces and other treasures. Built on the site where

The Chapel of San José.

ing. A Plateresque staircase leads up to the Archives, where the invaluable documents and works kept here include the city standard, dating back to the 15th century, and a painting by Juan Espinal of Saints Justa and Rufina, martyrs of the Triana district, dating back to 1760.

The famous, bustling **Calle de las Sierpes** has its origin in Plaza de San Francisco. The bars and terraces of

PET MARKET IN PLAZA DE LA ALFALFA

Every Sunday morning, peaceful Plaza de la Alfalfa, near Plaza del Salvador, is transformed into a veritable beehive of activity. A busy market selling pets and domestic animals attracts many visitors to the square, whether to buy or just to look. The most popular amongst the fauna here are birds, but we can also find exotic fish, dogs, cats, turtles, lizards and silkworms. The square's name is due to the fact that hay was once sold here.

Church of El Divino Salvador.

a mosque formerly stood, the church contains part of the Moorish patio of ablutions and the minaret. Opposite is the **Church and Hospital of San Juan de Dios (17)**, founded in the 16th century and also known as the Church and Hospital of Nuestra Señora de Paz.

The **Palace of the Condesa de Lebrija (18),** one of the finest of Sevillian palaces, stands in Calle Cuna. Built in the 15th and 16th centuries, the palace contains many Roman pieces, mostly from the ruins of Italica. Opposite is the **Former University**, founded in the 13th century and now the Academy of Fine Arts.

Palace of the Countess of Lebrija.

Calle Laraña and Calle Imagen lead to **Plaza de San Pedro (19)**, where two Gothic-Mudejar buildings stand: the Church of San Pedro and the Convent of Santa Inés. Further on, in **Plaza de los Terceros (20)** is the **Church of Santa Catalina**, another Gothic-Mudejar building which stands on the site of a mosque from which are conserved the *mihrab* and minaret. In nearby Calle Sol is the entrance to the **Church of Los Terceros**, dating back to the 17th century, with façade in American Colonial style.

The **Las Dueñas Palace (21)**, in Calle Las Dueñas, is a 15th-century house whose composition wisely combines the Mudejar, Gothic and Plateresque styles. Over the main entrance is an 18th-century coat of arms, whilst the lovely garden outside was once occupied by stables and a riding school. Particularly interesting is the main courtyard, decorated with Gothic plasterwork and a Plateresque balustrade. The palace, which once belonged to the dukes of Montijo, is the birthplace of the poets Antonio and Manuel Machado, sons of a high-standing employee of the duke. The site now belongs to the House of Alba, and written permission is required to visit the palace.

Calle Bustos de Tavera leads to **Plaza de San Marcos (22).** Various religious buildings stand in the vicinity of this square: the Church of San Marcos, the Convent of Santa Isabel and the Convent of Santa Paula, this last possessing an excellent collection of

Church of San Pedro.

Church of Santa Catalina.

Las Dueñas Palace, and partial view of the Church of San Marcos.

carvings, paintings and other objects of religious art. Calle San Luis leads directly to La Macarena. Along the way, we can admire the **Church of San Luis (23),** another outstanding Sevillian baroque church.

La Macarena (24) is, nowadays, one of the most colourful districts in Seville, and one which has best conserved its traditional air. Here we find part of the old city **walls** built by the Almoravides. This section runs from the Church of San Hermenegildo, beside Ronda de Capuchinos, to the Arch of La Macarena. The Church of San Hermenegildo contains the **Puerta de Córdoba**, a Moorish gate with horseshoe arch. According to legend, Ferdinand III, the Holy, entered Seville through this gate,

Walls and the Andalusian Parliament building.

Arch and Basilica of La Macarena. The Return of Our Lady during Holy Week.

disguised as a Moor, to inspect the city before conquering it. The old walls were demolished in the mid-19th century, apart from this section, conserved as a historical reminder.

The **Arch of La Macarena** corresponds to the old Almoravide city gate, or "Bab-al-Markina", altered to take the form we see today in the 19th century. Opposite stand the Basilica of La Macarena the former Hospital de la Sangre, since 1992 the seat of the **Andalusian Parliament**. This is an enormous Renaissance-style building organised around four courtyards. The former church in the hospital built by Hernán Ruiz in 1560, is now used as a debating chamber.

The **Basilica of La Macarena** was built between 1941 and 1946 in neo-baroque style, according to plans drawn up by Aurelio Gómez Millán. The basilica houses one of Seville's most-prized treasures, the image of Our Lady of Hope, La Macarena, as well as other magnificent statuary, including Our Lady of the Rosary, carved in the 18th century and attributed to Pedro Duque Cornejo, and the Christ of the Sentence, by Felipe Morales Nieto in 1654.

Calle Parra and Calle Feria are the main thoroughfares in La Macarena district. Since medieval times, the **Feria Market** has taken place each Thursday in Calle Feria and sur-

LA VIRGEN DE LA MACARENA

The statue of Our Lady of Hope, La Macarena, which stands over the high altar in the basilica of the same name, is always seen richly dressed in gold and silver. The author of this fine work is unknown, though it is attributed to Luisa Roldán, "La Roldana". Early on Good Friday morning, when the image is brought out to lead the procession, the square outside the basilica is filled with the passion of religious fervour. To cries of "Guapa!" (beautiful!) the paso, or float, carrying Our Lady crosses the city to the cathedral. The museum installed in the Treasure Room contains objects pertaining to this popular Hermandad, brotherhood, founded in 1595 and which performed its first station of penitence 1624. These treasures include, particularly, the rich mantles and jewels worn by Our Lady, as well as several trajes de luces, "suits of light", donated by famous bullfighters.

Market stalls in Calle de la Feria and Alameda de Hércules.

Church of Jesús del Gran Poder.

rounding area, when the streets are lined with stalls selling a vast range of wares. The **Alameda de Hércules (25),** antechamber to the San Vicente and San Lorenzo districts, is a very busy avenue on Sundays, when a popular weekly flea market takes place. At one end of the avenue are two Roman columns

with the statues of Hercules and Julius Caesar.

This route ends at the **Church of Jesús del Gran Poder (26),** a visit giving us the opportunity to admire the statue of Jesús del Gran Poder, Jesus of the Great Power, carved by Juan de Mesa in 1620, and one of the most deeply venerated in Seville.

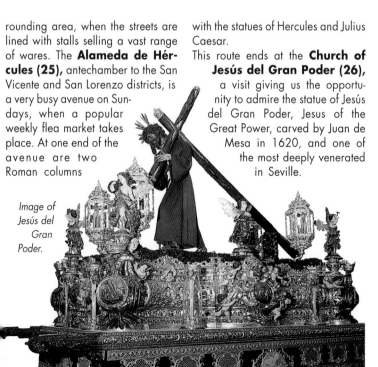

Image of Jesús del Gran Poder.

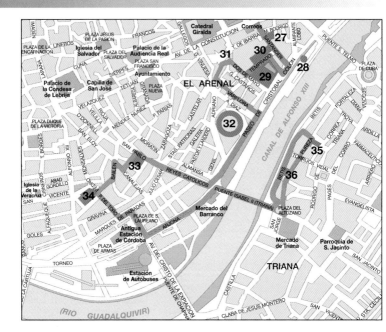

4. ALONG THE GUADALQUIVIR AND THE MUSEUM OF FINE ARTS

27.- The Mint. 28.- Torre del Oro. 29.- Teatro de la Maestranza. 30.- Hospital de la Caridad. 31.- Arch of El Postigo. 32.- Real Maestranza Bullring. 33.- Church of La Magdalena. 34.- Museum of Fine Arts. 35.- Church of Santa Ana. 36.- Chapel of Los Marineros.

Night view of the River Guadalquivir and the Triana bridge.

This route begins in Avenida de la Constitución at its crossing with Calle Santander. Adjoining the walls of the
Alcázar, the city walls, which formerly
protected Seville against attack from the
south, once followed the lay of this street,
extending down to the Torre del Oro
by the river. Still standing, half-hidden
amongst the buildings, are two more of
its turrets: the **Torre Abdelaziz**, named
after a Moorish prince, at the starting-
point of this route, and the octagonal
Torre de la Plata, which stands in
Calle Santander on the corner with Calle
Temprado. Go into the car park in Calle
Santander for an overall view.

As its layout reveals, the former **Mint**
("Casa de la Moneda") **(27)** once
housed a series of buildings with streets
and patios. This was originally the site
of the royal boatyards, until Philip II
ordered the construction of this enormous edifice through which passed the
immense treasure brought to Spain from
the New World. The site has now been
converted into an exhibition centre.

The **Torre del Oro (28)** has become
one of Seville's most emblematic
images. This is an Almohade fortifica-
tion with a dodecahedral ground plan,
built in the early-13th century, though
the smaller tower which crowns it is an
addition dating back to 1760. Its
name ("Tower of Gold") is due to the
fact that it was formerly covered by gilt
tiles. Connected by a thick chain across
the river to another tower, now lost, the
Torre del Oro served as a watchtow-
er over ships going up and down the
Guadalquivir. It now houses a **Mar-
itime Museum** whose exhibits evoke
Seville's history as a river port.

It was from the **River Guadalquivir**
- *Betis* to the Romans and *Guad el Kevir*
to the Moors - that the conquistadors

Torre de la Plata.

Torre del Oro.

set out on their voyages, and the tower is a symbol of the period around the discovery of America. In the former Arenal district, the area which now surrounds the Real Maestranza Bullring, in days gone by the mariners' quarter of the city, were the boatyards where the vessels which sailed between the Old and New Worlds were built. Due to the fact that the river was constan flooding its banks, in the mid-20th cen tury it was rechannelled away from it: path through the city centre. The Guadalquivir is crossed by a numbe of **bridges**. As part of this route we shall see: the Isabel II bridge, bette known as the Triana bridge, openec in 1852 to replace the former Las Bar

Triana bridge.

Teatro de la Maestranza.

Hospital of La Caridad: main courtyard, church front and the monument to Miguel de Mañara, the institution's principal benefactor.

cas bridge, until then the only point of communication between the two sides of the river; the San Telmo bridge, built between 1925 and 1931, and a drawbridge until the 1960s; and the Chapina bridge, completed in 1991.

From the Torre del Oro, we continue our route along Paseo de Cristóbal Colón. A new building stands out here: the **Teatro de la Maestranza (29),** an enormous circular theatre seating 1,800 spectators. The building was designed by the architects Aurelio del Pozo and Luis Marín de Terán.

Taking Calle Dos de Mayo now, we come to Calle de Temprado,

where we find the main entrance to the **Hospital of La Caridad (30).** This institution, which still functions as an old people's home, is one of the most privileged artistic spaces in the entire city, for it houses a magnificent art collection including masterpieces on the

theme of death and mercy by Valdés Leal and Murillo. Don Miguel de Mañara (1627-1679), who devoted his life to the institution after leading a dissolute life, directed work on the hospital and church, which is dedicated to Saint George, and personally designed the iconographic programme which has given the monument such renown.

Nearby is the **Arch of El Postigo (31),** also known as the Postigo del Aceite ("Oil Gate"), its name reminding us of the importance of the oil trade in Seville since Roman times. The design and foundations are due to the Almoravides, who built it as a prolongation of the city walls. It was altered during the 16th century to shape its present appearance. On one side, opened into

Arch of El Postigo: rear, and partial view of the decoration on the other façade.

Plaza del Cabildo.

Aerial view of the Real Maestranza bullring.

the wall, is a tiny chapel containing the image of the Pura y Limpia Concepción de la María Santísima.

At the end of Calle Dos de Mayo, a little passage, Pasaje de los Seises, leads to **Plaza del Cabildo**, a lovely arcaded square. A stamp and coin collectors' market takes place here on Sunday mornings.

Passing through the streets of the former Arenal district, with their shops and bars serving exquisite tapas, we return once more to Paseo de Cristóbal Colón. Our route takes in two interesting **chapels: La Carretería and El Baratillo**. The first is in Calle Varflora, and was founded by the coopers' and waggoners' guild. In it are venerated the images of the Cristo de la Salud and Nuestra Señora del Mayor Dolor. The second is in Calle Adriano and contains the images of Nuestra Señora de la Piedad and El Cristo de

la Misericordia, which is brought out for the Holy Week processions.

The **Maestranza Bullring (32)** is considered one of the most prestigious arenas devoted to the art of bullfighting. Designed by Vicente San Martín, it was built in the 18th century and restored

Real Maestranza bullring: the main entrance, or Puerta del Príncipe.

in the mid-19th. This is a magnificent, spacious and pleasant stadium, the ideal setting for demonstrations of tauromachy. The site also has a museum and a library. There are many keen, expert bullfighting fans amongst the people of Seville, for not in vain has its arena has been graced by some of the greatest *toreros* in bullfighting history. Not only that, but the city is the proud birthplace of such great masters of the art as Pepe-Hillo, Espartero, Belmonte, Gitanillo de Triana, Joselito, Cagancho and Chicuelo. The bullfighting season begins in

HOMAGE TO THE MASTERS OF BULLFIGHTING

In the San Fernando cemetery in the north of the city, lie several great maestros in the art of bullfighting. Manuel García, "El Espartero" (1865-1894) is buried in a magnificent pantheon, designed by Manuel Martínez, featuring a split pillar, symbolising this matador's life, cut off in its very youth, enveloped by a bullfighter's cape, or capote. The mortal remains of José Gómez Ortega, "Joselito" (1895-1920) also lie here, in one of the most beautiful pantheons in Spain. Carved by Mariano Benlliure in 1922, the sculpture over the tomb shows a group of men, cast in bronze, carrying the torero's body his face, shroud and pillow, in contrast, sculpted from Carrara marble. The figures represented in this work include the famed breeder of bulls Eduardo Miura and another bullfighter, Ignacio Sánchez Mejías. Joselito's brother, Rafael Gómez Ortega, "Rafael el Gallo" (1882-1969), another outstanding matador, also lies in this mausoleum.

Just opposite is a bronze statue of Francisco Rivera "Paquirri" (1948-1984), standing on a magnificent stone over the famous bullfighter's grave. The statue shows Paquirri in his full regalia, demonstrating one of his passes. Another elegant tomb is that of Manolo González (1929-1987), whilst that of Juan Belmonte (1892-1962) is as austere as he is said to have been himself, comprising four great blocks of unpolished marble. Other famous bullfighters whose mortal remains lie in the San Fernando cemetery include Manuel García "Maera" (1896-1921), "Fuentes Bejarano" (1902-1999) and Francisco Vega de los Reyes "Gitanillo de Triana" (1903-1931).

Tombs of Joselito and Paquirri.

Church of La Magdalena.

Seville each year with a *corrida* on Resurrection Sunday, which is followed by those of the April Fair - the city's most renowned bullfights – Corpus Christi and the Virgen de los Reyes, as well as the summer *novilladas* (bullfights with young bulls and novice *toreros*).

Taking first Calle Reyes Católicos and then Calle San Pablo, we come to the **Church of La Magdalena (33),** another outstanding exponent of the baroque style in Seville. It was built on the site of a late-17th-century Gothic-Mudejar church by Leonardo de Figueroa. The most interesting features in this church include the high altarpiece, the colourful tiles, the carvings and paintings by Zurbarán, Valdés Leal, Pedro Roldán and Lucas Valdés, amongst others.

We now take Calle Bailén to Plaza del Museo, where we find the **Museum of Fine Arts (34).** The museum is housed in a former convent which was rebuilt in the 17th century. The category and quantity of the works to be seen here make it Spain's second most important art museum, surpassed only by the Prado in Madrid. Besides paintings, the museum also houses collections of sculptures, ceramics and furniture. Some of the outstanding col-

Museum of Fine Arts.

"Souls in Purgatory" (1636), by Alonso Cano.

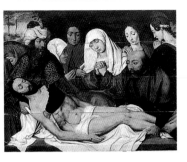

"Holy Burial" (h. 1560), an anonymous work from the Flemish School.

lections include the section devoted to the Seville School, featuring works by Pacheco, Alonso Cano, Herrera, Zurbarán, Roelas, Murillo and Valdés Leal, these last two founders of the Seville Academy. The collection of 19th-century art is equally extensive and valuable, including works by both Spanish and international artists. Particularly interesting in this category are

"Canon Cristóbal Suárez de Rivera", by Velázquez.

Room containing works by Murillo in the former convent church.

the works by Gonzalo de Bilbao, author of *"Las Cigarreras"* (The Cigarette Makers). This exceptional art museum also boasts a Greco and several works by Velazquez. The interior of the building is organised around three baroque-style porticoed patios. The main exhibition room occupies the old church, which has a single nave and a ground plan in the form of a Latin cross.

Heading back towards the river, the Isabel II Bridge leads us to the **Triana district**. Settled since ancient times, its name appears to refer to the Emperor Trajan, transformed into *Tarayanah* by the Moors. It was founded as an extension of Seville on the other side of the river, joined to the city proper by a single moving bridge made up of rafts, but Triana has always guarded its own peculiar identity jealously. It is a mariners' quarter par excellence: Rodri-

FLAMENCO

Seville is, with Jerez de la Frontera (Cádiz province), the leading cradle of Flamenco art, singing and dancing. The exact origins of this musical genre are unknown, but Flamenco's roots go back to the Middle Ages. Its principal exponents have always been Gypsies, whose music and dances absorbed influences from Andalusian Moorish folklore and Jewish and Christian elements. However, it was not until the 18th century that Flamenco began to take shape as the artform we now know, gradually emerging as the most representative expressive genre in Andalusian culture. Sevillanas, naturally, are the most typical and popular dances in the Andalusian capital. This dance, along with others, and Flamenco's artists' mastery of singing, guitar playing and hand-clapping, can be appreciated at one or other of the many tablaos all over the city. These Flamenco theatres abound particularly in the Santa Cruz and Triana districts. Triana is particularly recommended for those interested in hearing the cante jondo, for it is the cradle of many of the greatest Flamenco singers. Apart from the April Fair, the key date in the music-lover's diary should be the Flamenco Art Biennial, which takes place in September and October.

*Aficionados should also visit the **Museum of Flamenco Dance** in Calle Manuel Rojas Marcos, not far from the cathedral. Artistic direction at this new museum, opened in spring 2006, is in the hands of the celebrated dancer and choreographer Cristina Hoyos, who is also the director of the museum's dance school.*

go of Triana accompanied Columbus on board the Pinta and was the first European to sight America. Here, too, crews were recruited to sail to the New World, among them that of the celebrated Magellan expedition. Triana's still-thriving pottery industry goes back over one thousand years, moreover, whilst the district is also the cradle of great Flamenco *cantaores* as well as *toreros*.

Chapel of El Carmen.

The Triana Bridge, or Isabel II Bridge, leads to **Plaza del Altozano**. This square was built in the 19th century after the demolition of the old San Jorge Castle. Here is the **Chapel of El Carmen**, popularly known due to its shape as "El Mechero" - the cigarette lighter. It was built in 1926 by the architect Aníbal González. There is also a **monument to Belmonte**, the renowned bullfighter who made his debut at the Maestranza Bullring in 1910. A peculiar view of this arena can be obtained through the hole in the statue's chest.

Monument to Juan Belmonte.

The main thoroughfares in the Triana district have their starting-point in Plaza del Altozano: these are Calle San Jacinto, Calle Betis and Calle Castilla. Calle Betis, lined with pavement cafés, commands splendid views over the city. In Plaza de la Sacrada Familia, known as "La Plazuela", stands the **Church of Santa Ana (35),** until the 19th century the cathedral of Triana. It was founded by Alphonse X and contains elements from the Gothic to the baroque.

Church of Santa Ana.

The high altarpiece, presided over by Saint Ann, the Madonna and the Child, is the most interesting element in the church. In nearby Calle Pureza is the **Chapel of Los Marineros (36),** which contains the statue of the Virgin de la Esperanza de Triana, a statue of Our Lady venerated by the entire population of the district. The best way of getting to know Triana is to wander around its streets, discovering charming patios adorned with colourful flowers, typical houses and traditional old shops.

Virgen de la Esperanza de Triana.

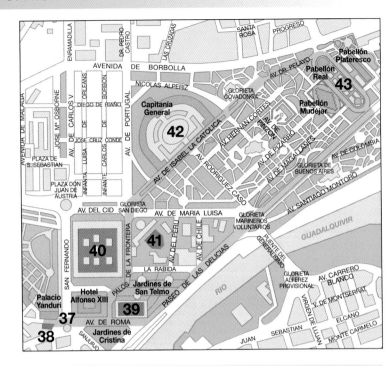

5. FROM THE PUERTA DE JEREZ TO MARIA LUISA PARK

37.- Puerta de Jerez. 38.- Chapel of Maese Rodrigo. 39.- Palace of San Telmo. 40.- University (former the Tobacco Factory). 41.- Teatro Lope de Vega. 42.- Plaza de España. 43.- Plaza de América.

The Jerez Gate, or **Puerta de Jerez (37)** formerly gave passage through the walls to the vineyards. Demolished in 1864, the site is now occupied by a fine fountain, built in the early-20th century and designed by Delgado Brackenbury. The square is lined by interesting buildings: the French-style **Palace of Yanduri**, the house known as the **Casa de los Guardiola**, its style reminiscent of the Renaissance, and the **Hotel de Alfonso XIII**, one of the great works undertaken on the occasion of the 1929 Spanish-American Exhibition, a wise mixture of two very different styles closely linked to the artistic history of Seville, the Mudejar and the baroque. The architectural wealth of the Puerta de Jerez site is completed by a fourth building, the **Chapel of Maese Rodrigo (38),** a small Gothic-Mudejar church which belonged to the original University of Seville, lost as part of the extension of Avenida de la Constitución. The chapel boasts a magnificent display of gilt *azulejos* (glazed tiles) and a fine altarpiece with paintings by Alejo Fer-

Fountain in the Jerez Gate, and the Hotel Alfonso XIII.

nández. It also features a fine main or toral arch.

The construction of the **Palace of San Telmo (39)** began in 1682. This palace features a fine Churrigueresque

Guardiola House.

Yanduri Palace.

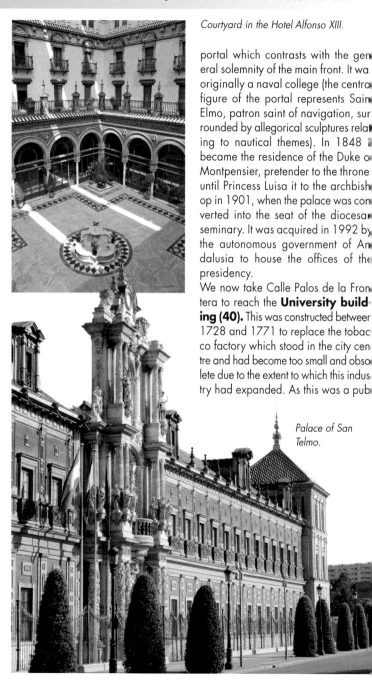

Courtyard in the Hotel Alfonso XIII.

portal which contrasts with the general solemnity of the main front. It was originally a naval college (the central figure of the portal represents Saint Elmo, patron saint of navigation, surrounded by allegorical sculptures relating to nautical themes). In 1848 it became the residence of the Duke of Montpensier, pretender to the throne until Princess Luisa it to the archbishop in 1901, when the palace was converted into the seat of the diocesan seminary. It was acquired in 1992 by the autonomous government of Andalusia to house the offices of the presidency.

We now take Calle Palos de la Frontera to reach the **University building (40).** This was constructed between 1728 and 1771 to replace the tobacco factory which stood in the city centre and had become too small and obsolete due to the extent to which this industry had expanded. As this was a pub

Palace of San Telmo.

University building and courtyard, former the Tobacco Factory.

lic building, it was designed in the form of a citadel, explaining why it contains a prison, moat and drawbridge. The tobacco industry was then very powerful and the factory therefore had a permanent guard over it to prevent smuggling and the constant black marketeering. The "Fábrica de Tabacos" enjoyed a monopoly in the production of tobacco and was for many years the most prosperous industry in Seville, employing the biggest workforce, amongst them Carmen, the popular cigar-maker who inspired Merimée's novel of the same name. The building takes the shape of an enormous rectangle measuring 250 by 180 metres and was formerly divided into two areas: the residential section and the factory itself.

Between the University and María Luisa Park is the **Teatro Nacional Lope de Vega (41),** another of the

Teatro Lope de Vega.

CARMEN, THE CIGARETTE GIRL

Carmen has become one of Seville's most popular characters, her story told in book, film, theatre and opera form. This cigarette girl worked at the powerful Real Fábrica de Tabacos de Sevilla, where it is said that three-quarters of all the cigars smoked in Europe were made. One day, in a dispute with one of her fellow workers, Carmen stabs a girl, then bewitches the corporal, José, sent to arrest her so that he joins her gang of smugglers. Carmen then leaves infatuated soldier for a bullfighter. Desperate, José finally kills his beloved. There is a statue representing Carmen just outside the bullring.

many works undertaken for the 1929 Spanish-American Exhibition. Its principal artifice was Vicente Traver, who succeeded Aníbal González as director of the projects carried out as part of that magnum celebration.

Though the great event was postponed on various occasions before it was finally staged - it was originally due to take place in 1914, but the outbreak of the First World War prevented its inauguration, and the nomination of Seville

María Luisa Park: Isleta de los Patos.

María Luisa Park: Glorieta de las Palomas kiosk, partial view of the fountain of La Glorieta de las Palomas, and partial view of the Fountain of the Lions.

as host city brought with it controversy between different currents of thought as to what architectural style and signs of identity should be employed - it is undeniable that the city opened up a new space, until then outside the walls, dominated by extensive gardens. The fountain of the **Glorieta de San Diego** was built at the main entrance to the site. Beyond it stretches the leafy marvel which is the **María Luisa Park**, a particularly pleasant spot during the hot summer months.

María Luisa Park was donated to the city by Princess Doña Luisa in 1893 and shortly after was converted into the site for the 1929 world fair, a restructuring involving the

construction of pavilions and squares, as well as fountains and **glorietas** (kiosks). The most popular of these glorietas is the one dedicated to the Sevillian poet Gustavo Adolfo Bécquer, by Coullaut Varela in 1912. In it, the three women symbolise the three states of love - hope, surrender and loss - and the two angels, the love which wounds and wounded love. Several of the original **pavilions** are still standing, particularly along Paseo de las Delicias. Most interesting are: the Mexican pavilion, its architecture influenced by Mayan

Monument to Gustavo Adolfo Bécquer.

art; that of Guatemala, its exterior tiled by *azulejos*; and the Peruvian Pavilion, with lovely wooden balconies. Part of the park extends along the river, and this stretch of the Guadalquivir contains three **bridges**: that of Alfonso XIII, a drawbridge opened in 1926; that of the Fifth Centenary, characterised by its modern forms; and that of El Generalísimo, better known of the Puente Nuevo, inaugurated in 1968.

In the kiosk known as the Glorieta de los Marineros Voluntarios stands a **monument to Juan Sebastián Elcano**, who disembarked in the port of Seville in 1522 after becoming the first navigator to sail around the world. Here, too, is the building known as the Queen's sewing room, or **Costurero de la Reina**, now the city tourist information office, a tiny castle that once formed part of the grounds of the Palace of San Telmo.

The French landscape gardener Forestier took part in the work of organising the gardens, redesigning them completely with the only condition that he should respect the original layout of

Guatemala, Mexico and Peru pavilions.

Fifth Centenary bridge.

the orchard donated by Doña Luisa. Employing water as one of the principal elements, Forestier sought to increase the effects of light and the horizontal qualities of the park, as well as planting an extensive variety of vegetation.

Nevertheless, the most interesting features of María Luisa Park are Plaza de España and Plaza de América.

Glorieta de los Marineros Voluntarios: monument to Juan Sebastián el Cano and, in the background, the Queen's Sewing Room (Costurero de la Reina).

Aerial view of Plaza de España.

Plaza de España (42) consists of a 200-meter diameter semicircle culminating in two high, stylised towers at either end. An artificial canal flows in the interior, crossed by little bridges with a Venetian air and decorated with tiles. On the benches lined around the semicircle are represented all the Spanish provinces in alphabetical order, each identified by its coat of arms, a map of the province and by symbols alluding to its histo-

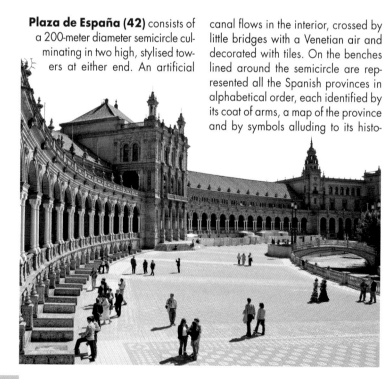

Views of Plaza de España.

Royal Pavilion.

The Plateresque Pavilion, which houses the Archaeological Museum.

The Mudejar Pavilion (Museum of Popular Arts and Customs).

ry. Above, a series of medallions depict personalities linked to the history of Spain since earliest times. In the interior of the central building is a two-storey porticoed patio. The materials used are brick decorated with fine ceramics. The square, which was designed by Aníbal González, has now become an outstanding symbol of the city of Seville.

Plaza de América (43) contains three pavilions, exponents of three different tendencies: the Mudejar, the Gothic and the Renaissance, styles which also predominate in the rest of the works in the park. Once again, Aníbal González was chief amongst those working to design and build this square. The **Pabellón Real** (Royal Pavilion) is a building in Flamboyant Gothic style. The **Pabellón**

Plateresco, or Renacentista (Plateresque or Renaissance Pavilion) now houses the **Archaeological Museum**, one of the leading museums of its kind in Spain, its collections including the extraordinary *Carambolo Treasure*, a magnificent jewellery collection going back to the times of Tartessian culture (6th century BC). The museum also contains many pieces from Roman times, including sculptures of Hermes, Diana, Venus, Trajan and Hadrian. Finally, the **Pabellón Mudéjar** has been the seat of the **Museum of Popular Arts and Customs** since 1973. This museum offers visitors an excellent opportunity of seeing a range of objects in daily use in Seville province (costumes, furniture and other utensils) from Moorish times to the present.

La Chapina bridge.

6. ISLA DE LA CARTUJA

44.- La Cartuja. 45.- Puerta de Triana Cultural Space. 46.- Isla Mágica. 47.- Alamillo Park. 48.- Olympic Stadium.

This last route leads us to discover the area that served as the venue for the Universal Exposition, or Expo, in 1992. The site receives the name "isla", island, because it is bounded by two branches of the River Guadalquivir, and "de la Cartuja" because the Carthusian monastery was practically the only building that existed here prior to its development for the Expo. The organisation of this great event entailed not only the entire development of this zone, but also considerable improvements to the city's infrastructure, including the construction of the High Speed Train service (AVE), the new airport and ring roads, and four **bridges** over the river (Cachorro or Chapina, La Cartuja, La Barqueta and El Alamillo). The first two are the most spectacular. La Barqueta, a suspension bridge 235 metres long and 11 wide, was built by the engineers Juan J. Arenas and Marcos J. Pantaleón, whilst El Alamillo, with its harp shape and single arm supporting its entire weight, was designed by Santiago Calatrava.

Taking one of these bridges, La Cartuja pedestrian bridge, we come, firstly, to the site of the former Monastery of Santa María de las Cuevas, better known as **La Cartuja (44)**. Christopher Columbus stayed on various occasions at this monastery, founded in the

La Barqueta bridge.
El Alamillo bridge.

Former Monastery of Santa María de las Cuevas, La Cartuja.

15th century, sharing the theories that would lead him to discover the New World with the monks. The monumental sight was also where the monarch stayed when visiting Seville. The Carthusian monks stayed here until 1836, when they were expelled under the law of disentailment concerning the Church's goods. Many of the works the monastery once housed, including many of the most outstanding masterpieces produced by the Seville School, are now exhibited at the Museum of Fine Arts. After disentailment, the site was converted into a ceramic factory, which it remained until 1982, and the tall chimneys from this factory are still conserved. The monastery was used as the Royal Pavilion for the 1992 Expo, and now houses the Andalusian Institute for Historical Heritage, the office of the vice chancellor of the International University of Andalusia and the **Andalusian**

La Cartuja: main entrance.

View of the CAAC gardens, with the chimneys from the old ceramic factory.

Centre for Contemporary Art (CAAC), which organises temporary exhibitions as well as containing a representative collection of works by the most outstanding Andalusian contemporary artists. The most interesting of the old monastery buildings are the Priory, the chapel known as La Capilla de Afuera, the Chapter Room and the Mudejar cloister.

The **Puerta de Triana Cultural Space (45)**, near La Cartuja, is a site containing such attractions as an Omnimax cinema, the Navigation Pavilion, the ship *Victoria* (a replica of a 16th-century vessel) and a tower commanding fine views of the city and surrounding countryside.

On the way to Isla Mágica and further north, we can see many modern buildings, some part of the 1992 legacy, others more recent additions. These include: the **World Trade Center**, with its use of advanced bioclimatic tech-

Gardens of the Puerta de Triana Cultural Space.

World Trade Center.

Canal Sur broadcasting company headquarters.

designed by Santiago Calatrava; and the **Auditorium**, an open air facility with marble fronts, built according to plans drawn up Eleuterio Población Knappe.

The **Isla Mágica theme park (46)** is one of Seville's most outstanding attractions. The park is divided into six thematic areas recreating the voyages and feats of 16th-century explorers. In "Sevilla, Puerto de Indias" (Seville, Port of the Indies) you can learn to be a daring adventurer at the School for

The open-air Auditorium

nology and indoor garden, designed by Antonio Vázquez de Castro; the **Canal Sur building**, headquarters of Andalusia's broadcasting company, the work of the architect Juan Ruesga; the **Torretriana** tower by F.J. Sáenz de Oiza; the **Kuwait Pavilion**,

The Torretriana tower.

Explorers and make a crossing of the lake. In the "Quetzal" area, visitors can ride the Ciklón, a Mayan disk that shoots up to a height of 14 metres, spinning wildly around, and brave the wrath of the gods in the Furia de los Dioses, an Odyssey with ten thrilling challenges. In the "Puerta de América", or Gateway to America, area, the most popular attraction is the Anaconda, a big dipper with water chute over trunks. Even bigger, though, is the Jaguar big dipper in the "Amazonia" area, with 360-degree turns and vertiginous drops. Another exciting ride in this area is the Iguazú, in which visitors take a raft over a great waterfall. One of the shows we can see in the pirate's den, or "Guarida de los Piratas", features a mutiny, whilst the main attractions in "Eldorado" are the aviary and the "Orinoco Rapids", nearly 500 metres of rafting

Isla Mágica: recreation of a 16th-century caravel.

Isla Mágica: two big dippers, the Anaconda and the Jaguar, and the "Orinoco Rapids"

aboard a rubber dinghy. Finally, "El Balcón de Andalucía" contains scale reproductions of the one hundred most representative landscapes and monuments in the region.

There is space, too, on Isla de la Cartuja, for parks and gardens, all opened for the 1992 Expo. Here we find the Gardens of The Americas and of the Guadalquivir, the Park of the Discoveries and, at the northern end of the "island", the **Alamillo Park (47)**, a recreation of the Mediterranean wood-land environment. Covering 47 hectares, this is the largest park on Isla de la Cartuja.

There are also several sports facilities at the northern end of Isla de la Cartuja, including the **Olympic Stadium (48)**. The architects, Antonio Cruz and Antonio Ortiz, built part of the stadium below ground level to palliate the environmental impact caused by such a huge site. Officially inaugurated in 1999, Seville's finest sports facility seats 60,000 spectators.

The Olympic Stadium.

SPORTS FACILITIES

Seville's best-known sports facilities are the San Pablo Sports Palace and the Ramón Sánchez Pizjuán and Manuel Ruiz de Lopera football stadiums. The San Pablo is where the city's basketball team, Caja San Fernando, play their home matches in the Spanish Association of Basketball Club's ACB championship, the equivalent of the First Division, as well as European League and other international competitions. The main front of Ramón Sánchez Pizjuán Stadium, home of Sevilla Fútbol Club, features an enormous mosaic with the club coat of arms in the centre, surrounded by those of clubs from all over the world. The local rivals, Real Betis Balompié, play their home match-es before a passionate, fiercely-loyal crowd at the Manuel Ruiz de Lopera Stadium, known as the Benito Villamarín Stadium until it was officially rebap-tised on 31 December 2001.

The Manuel Ruiz de Lopera and Ramón Sánchez Pizjuán football stadiums.

CONTENTS

EDITORIAL FISA ESCUDO DE ORO, S.A.
Tel: 93 230 86 00
www.eoro.com

I.S.B.N. 84-378-1857-5
Legal Dep. B. 24259-2006